Anonymous

The Barnums of Business

The Departmental Stores and their Relation to Trade, Property and Wages

Anonymous

The Barnums of Business
The Departmental Stores and their Relation to Trade, Property and Wages

ISBN/EAN: 9783337715052

Printed in Europe, USA, Canada, Australia, Japan

Cover: Foto ©Suzi / pixelio.de

More available books at **www.hansebooks.com**

...THE...

Barnums of Business

The Departmental Stores and Their Relation to Trade, Property and Wages.

BY MACK

A reprint of the articles on departmental stores that have appeared in TORONTO SATURDAY NIGHT *from February 13 to April 24, 1897.*

———

TORONTO:
THE SHEPPARD PUBLISHING COMPANY, Ltd.
1897.

MONOPOLIZED.

From The Ram's Horn.

NO. I.—THE QUESTION OF POSTAGE ON NEWS-PAPERS IN RELATION TO CENTRALIZATION OF TRADE.

AT the meeting of the Press Association held here recently the editor of a country paper said that it was only the city publishers who favored the proposal to charge postage on newspapers. This is not quite true, because many country papers have declared in favor of paying postage, but it is so nearly true that we may call it a fact. It is, however, a peculiar fact, and any peculiar fact is worth looking into. Why should a city newspaper with a daily circulation of twenty or thirty thousand copies, ask the Government to charge postage on newspapers? It would mean a very heavy daily expenditure of money, and the man who asks it must see gain somewhere. The city publisher is not so rich that he does not know what to do with his money. He has other reasons for inviting postage, and he considers them good reasons. The question is, Should the country publisher aid or resist him? A postal rate that would cost $50 per annum for a thousand papers sent out every week, is proposed. This means about one dollar per thousand per issue. The city publisher then would pay on a daily circulation of twenty thousand copies the sum of $6,240 per annum in postage. The weekly paper with one thousand of a circulation would pay $50 per annum in postage. If there are ends to be gained worth $6,240 a year to the city publisher, the country publisher should consider it worth while to see whether the advantages would not be worth $50 a year to him.

It is an instinctive fear of an approaching danger that causes the city publisher to invite postage, but I think that not only future dangers, but evils already here, should cause country publishers to stand up in a row and

unanimously shout for postage. Type-setting
machines, fast presses, cheaper paper, and free
postage have caused the size of daily newspapers to double and the price of them to be
cut in half in the past four years. Evening
papers that cost three or four dollars a year
not long ago, are now selling for one dollar per
year, and are almost double their former size.
Immense papers from across the boundary
lines are coming in—great factory-made papers,
as cheap in merit as in price. The thing has
only begun. City publishers are unable to
decide where it will all end. They know that
they are being overwhelmed by a new tendency
towards bulk and cheapness, and that the
safety and credit of the publishing business
demand that some sort of a check must be
devised, some brake must be put on. On my
desk lies a thirty-two-column newspaper, containing only one column of live matter, the
rest being boiler-plate. The plan of this sheet
is to get a big advertisement for some departmental store or patent medicine firm, and send
out five or ten thousand copies free by mail to
approved addresses for a lump sum. This
represents the other evil—the fake newspaper
that competes with the legitimate daily. The
city publisher, then, seeing the evils that are
here and those that threaten, favors postage.

Not publishing a daily paper, I can be candid
as regards the rural press. It is perhaps safe
to say that for each copy of a daily paper that
went into the villages of Ontario four years
ago, there are now fifteen. The dollar daily
has only begun to get in its fine work. The
local paper can never be crowded out, you say
with much truth, for the local paper has a
powerful hold. But it is walking into an am-
bush. The editor of a village weekly if offered
an advertisement by a Toronto departmental
store wi'l refuse it in loyalty to local business
houses. But yet, refusing the revenue that

he could thus derive, he runs for nothing on errands for the departmental store by clubbing his paper with a dollar daily that contains nothing so conspicuous as the advertisement of the departmental store. By clubbing with and freely advertising the dollar daily, he places in the hands of his readers and the customers of his own advertisers an advertisement quoting cunning prices and instructing them how to do business by mail with the departmental store. Thus the mail carries free into his field the literature of the departmental stores of Toronto, and the mails carry also, for next to nothing, the merchandise of those institutions. The mail order business of one departmental store in Toronto runs weekly away up into many thousands of dollars. It is the competitor of every store in the province, and the scheme is only half developed as yet. Where will the local paper be when outside advertisers can cover its field in the dollar daily or the fifty-cent daily, and when the departmental stores have succeeded in smothering the local trade of all towns as the towns within touching distance of Toronto are already smothered? The props that keep up the local press will have been pulled away.

This matter of postage, then, is not one that interests only the country editor, but the country merchant, who, while postage of newspapers is free, is submitting to a tax that assists the departmental stores to place their bait under the noses of the people in every hamlet in Canada.

II.—RETAILERS MUST EITHER LINE UP FOR BATTLE OR LIE DOWN TO BE MASSACRED.

IT is my belief that if the men who run the great departmental stores in Toronto were to come together to draft a set of postal laws for the Dominion, they could scarcely suggest any alterations that would make the postal service of this country more completely subservient to their interests than it is now. The postal law permits newspapers to be carried free; and without free postage there could be no dollar daily newspaper crowding in, or being sent in to every town and village without any cost whatever, carrying the expansive and seductive advertisements of the mammoth stores of Toronto. Without free postage the fake newspapers that exist only for the advertisements they contain, could not be circulated. The parcel postage rate was fixed in order to meet the convenience of the public; it is being used as the distributing agency of a few monopolies in Toronto intent upon seizing the mercantile trade of all Canada.. The book postage rate was made lower still, so that knowledge might not be hampered in its movements; it is being used for nothing so much as for the bulky packages of departmental store catalogues which are sent out in tons to addresses in every town and township in English-speaking Canada.

Postmaster-General Mulock is known to be working on a revision of the postal laws. If the departmental store men are able to perceive any way or ways in which the postal service of Canada may be made to still more faithfully serve their interests, rest assured that those changes will be urged upon Hon. Mr. Mulock. It will be done adroitly. The arguments will be plausible. The voice of the petitioners will sound like the voice of the people. Therefore, those who believe that the mail cars of this country should not be the delivery

wagons of a few stores in Toronto and
Montreal, must stand up right now and make
vigorous protests. So far the departmental
stores have met with no resistance. They have
merely been yelled at. Such attacks as have
been made upon them by newspapers have
ceased when those papers secured advertising
contracts. Toronto has seen all the old-
established forms of trade shaken or over-
turned by a new shape of opposition, but she
has been unable to voice her alarm. The
silence of the press has misled the people in the
city and throughout the province.

TORONTO SATURDAY NIGHT would have
broken silence long ago, only that no plan of
action presented itself. Now, however, there
is work to be done. The interests of the people
require to be protected in the revision of the
postal laws, not only as regards newspaper
postage, but also parcel and book post. The
whole mail system of the Dominion, maintained at great cost by the nation, must not
become an arm in the vast organization of a
departmental store monopoly. It is almost
that now. There are projects on foot aiming
to make every mail clerk, postman and mail
driver in the land the errand boy and burden-
bearer of the departmental store.

The time has come when retailers must either
line up for battle or lie down to be massacred.
Every newspaper editor who is not securely
jailed in by his advertising manager should
break loose and set fire to local sentiment,
and every merchant who has trade to lose
should come forward to protect his business.

Talk about a National Policy! There is a
Personal Policy, anciently described as the law
of self-preservation, and the salvation of ten
thousand merchants and the business welfare
of a thousand towns depend upon the capacity
of these scattered persons to be wise and united
for once in defending their interests. In this

city there is a Retail Merchants' Association, organized specially to combat the departmental stores, and every storekeeper in Ontario should become a member of it. Two hundred and fifty of the best retail merchants of Toronto belong to this Association, for they know that a departmental store is a powerful organization and must be met by an organization yet more powerful.

Honest enterprise is commendable, but any one enterprise that destroys ten others should be very carefully examined to see if it is honest.

If it can be shown that the very people who are being financially destroyed by the departmental stores are taxed to make their extermination easy——

If it can be shown that the departmental stores have reduced the wages of working people in Toronto and in factories throughout the province without increasing the purchasing power of money as regards the real neces saries of life——

If it can be shown that departmental stores have arrested building operations and other lines of industrial activity in this and adjoining towns——

If it can be shown that a reputation for cheapness is gained by a clever manipulation of wares and words, and that the real profits of monopoly go to the monopolists——

If it can be shown, in short, that departmental stores aim at the overthrow of all the mercantile, financial and industrial conditions that at present prevail and the substitution of an entirely new order of things not provided for nor even dreamed of by those who framed the present municipal and commercial laws, does it not irresistibly follow that there must be new legislation suited to the new conditions? And if revolutionary changes are threatened, may not the multitude of people who will be prejudicially affected resist and prevent those changes?

The daily paper that derives ten thousand dollars a year from departmental stores is not likely to turn a too suspicious eye upon such good customers. The hope of the country is the provincial press, which has nothing to gain and everything to lose by these great, all-gobbling institutions. Last week I argued that country publishers should stand up in a row and shout for the imposition of postage upon newspapers. The dollar daily is the natural child of free postage, and it is the well paid and disguised emissary of the departmental store. Once upon a time the advertisements in a newspaper clung timidly to the reading matter—now the reading matter hides precariously in whatever holes and corners the advertisers have despised. The dollar daily is not the newspaper that was granted free transmission through the mails; it is an offspring of that privilege. The country publisher may write as eloquently as he pleases once a week in favor of supporting local merchants, but if he clubs with a dollar daily or booms it in his columns he defeats himself. The advertisement of the local merchant appears in the local paper and reaches the local public once a week. The dollar daily places the advertisement of the departmental store under the noses of the customers of the local merchant six times a week; and these advertisements are changed daily; they are large and attractive, written by men who do nothing else and draw large salaries for writing one seductive advertisement every day. What chance has the local merchant in so unequal contest? Dollar dailies will perish the very day that they are required to pay postage, and in no other way can they be restricted.

An out-of-town correspondent, an ex-publisher, writes as follows:

In your timely and sensible remarks on the news-paper postage and departmental store questions in the last SATURDAY NIGHT, do you not overlook one point in your calculation as to the cost of postage on the city dailies? You state that the city publisher on a daily circulation of 20,000 copies would on a certain proposed rate pay $6,240 per annum in postage. But is not the greater part of the city circulation sent in express parcels? Or sold by newsboys? What proportion of the daily circulation actually goes through the postoffice? Do not the country publishers know this, and does not this fact explain their attitude? There is no doubt as to the far-reaching effects of the big departmental store. Will not one result be: fewer stores in country towns and fewer local advertisers for the country paper?

ONLOOKER.

To the last question we answer: Undoubtedly. As regards the part played by express companies in the circulation of cheap dailies, it may be said that the mail bags do the important preliminary work. When a dollar daily is being introduced into a town or village, the mail carries the few copies that go there, but when the thing goes to its full length the big bundles are sent by express. But the rural parts that surround towns and support them cannot be reached by express, and the mail covers these. We have the report of the Postal Department showing that one daily paper used eighteen hundred mail bags in one month, or sixty-four bags per day. In the calculation made last week I referred to a circulation of twenty thousand sent through the mails at the rate of one cent per pound. Even if we estimated that a daily with twenty thousand of a circulation only sends seven thousand daily through the mails, this would mean an annual outlay of $2,184 for postage. That city publishers invite this tax should cause country publishers to enquire if there would not be advantage for them in paying a tax of $50 per annum.

Having now opened this question of departmental stores and their relation to the country at large, I shall next take up one particular phase of the subject.

WHEN a man dies and the man who lived next door comes forward and says, "He was a good neighbor," there remains very little more to be said about the deceased in the way of praise. No higher certificate of character could very well be given. The man next door had "neighbored" with him in the back yard as well as on the front stoop, and if there had been anything nasty about the late lamented gentleman the man next door would have found it out to his cost. A good neighbor is one who does not steal your wood, nor poison your dog, nor smash the fence for kindling, nor make noises in the night, nor let his hens into your flower-beds, nor tell tales of your private affairs. A good neighbor is one with whom you are on reciprocal terms in all the courtesies of life—exchange for each other's advantage all sorts of conveniences, doing for each other many thoughtful little things.

A good neighbor does not merely stand on his own lot and refrain from doing you injury. You work each other mutual good. If your house catches fire he rushes in and warns you. He piles in with an enthusiasm equal to your own to quench the fire or to save your goods from loss.

He does this because he knows you well, likes you and has your real welfare at heart. Moreover, your welfare and his own are inseparably locked together, because if your house is burned down his own will almost undoubtedly be consumed also. Even if his house is far enough away to be out of danger, the value of his home will be reduced if your house is replaced by a cellar full of ashes and burnt timbers. The proprietor of the departmental store is not your neighbor.

Ten years ago there were great stretches of

commons lying north, east and west of what was then the city of Toronto. Since then, these commons have been built up with residences and places of business. Take Spadina avenue north of Knox College, for instance. That was open country not long ago—now it is a town of itself. Those who own property there are interested in the values of lands and houses. Those who live there are interested in the conveniences of the neighborhood. The drug store is a convenience. If a member of the family takes ill in the night, you can go there and rouse the druggist from his sleep to get you what is needed. If you wish to find anyone's address you go to the drug store to consult the city directory. You use his telephone now and then ; you buy postage stamps there. He is a member of your church near by and contributes to its support. He pays local improvement taxes and helps to make the street smooth for your carriage or your bicycle. He is your neighbor. You are useful to each other in ways you do not pause to consider.

Yet when you go to a departmental store to buy your perfumes, or soaps, or patent medicines a few cents cheaper than he offers them, you destroy the vitality of your own neighborhood. If his business declines, he must reduce his expenditures ; he must give less to the local church and its schemes, less to local charities ; he must shut his hand. If he is forced to assign, the local butcher and baker get only 30c. on the dollar for what he owes them. Then they, too, must hedge and scrape to make up this loss. But perhaps you or your son or your brother may clerk in a downtown wholesale where that druggist had an account. That wholesale house gets only 30c. on the dollar from that druggist, and ten other druggists having similarly been forced to assign in ten other parts of the city, it follows that the wholesale house must assign also, and all its clerks and travelers be thrown out of employment. The trade cannot absorb them all. The rate of salaries is reduced by the fact that these expert applicants are trying to wedge in somewhere. One wholesale failure causes other houses to cut down expenses—they grow timid and parsimonious. They dismiss a couple of travelers. They double up work in the office and let men go. To follow through all their ramifications the consequences of these failures would be impossible, but it is safe to say this, that a tremor goes through every part of the business body of this city of Toronto.

But to get back to your locality. There is an empty building there now instead of a drug store. The drugs, the telephone, the postage stamps, the estimable citizen and his family have moved away. The locality is that much poorer, that much less convenient to live in, that much less important as a portion of the city; it is a limb that trails dependent upon the trunk of the town. The loan company that has had the vacant store thrown on its hands, resists any attempt to have the street repaved. Those who used to come from another quarter to that drug store, now go elsewhere—passing other bake shops, other grocery stores, other meat stores. Some day they pause and deal in one of these, and are perhaps lost to the locality as purchasers within its area.

The policy that can thus kill a drug store can kill off any other kind of local store, and the injury is almost as great. The concern that was patronized in preference to the local stores has no memory for faces. You may deal there twenty years, yet if you lose your situation and are penniless in the middle of winter you could not get a loaf of bread on credit. Whether you flourish or perish is all one to the unseen power that owns the departmental store. It recognizes only one face—the face of the Queen on coin of the realm.

Take a town fifty miles from Toronto. If you pay the local merchant ten dollars for an overcoat, perhaps he pays it to the doctor for attendance, he to the druggist for drugs, he to the butcher for meat, he to the farmer for mutton, he to a laborer for digging a well, he to another, and so that ten-dollar bill serves the purposes of trade in and around that town indefinitely. But if you send it away to a departmental store for an overcoat, that other overcoat lies on the local merchant's shelf, and that ten-dollar bill may never again enter your community.

The real value of this point lies in the fact that the profit in the sale of the overcoat goes to an institution in a distant city—an institution that has nothing in common with you--and that profit is lost to the merchant who helps to keep up your schools and churches. your sidewalks and roads, the man to whom you can appeal in an emergency to play the part of a neighbor.

In the year 1870 less than 19 per cent. of the population of Canada dwelt in cities, and in 1890 the rate had grown to nearly 29 per cent.

This change was largely due to the development of agricultural machinery no doubt, yet if rural Ontario is to be deprived of a large and ever-growing percentage of its people, and if on top of this the cities are to draw away from the dwindling towns and villages an ever-increasing share of their shrinking trade ; and if the cities, growing ever more populous and dominant in the trade of the whole province, are to contain only three or four mammoth stores instead of three or four hundred, have we not here all the materials for such a monopoly as the world has never seen ?

What is to prevent a dozen millionaires forming a company to operate a chain of stores from

one end of Canada to the other, with a total
capital of forty or fifty millions of dollars?
Once the city of Toronto is at the mercy of
three or four stores, it will be easy for them to
secretly unite whilst keeping up a sham fight
to deceive the public. Against such a tremendous combination of capital and against such
an organization, no new store could make any
headway. Having a monopoly here a move
could be made on, let us say, London. In order
to batter down all existing business houses
there, the millionaires' combine could put in an
enormous stock, advertise lavishly, and actually
sell goods for less than cost, and lose five hundred thousand dollars in crowding all opposition
aside. They would regard this as *the cost of
the franchise.* And it would be worth the
money.

Having conquered London and laid all
Western Ontario under tribute, the company
could speedily restore to capital account all
that the franchise had cost, and then, pursuing
the same tactics, Montreal, Winnipeg, Van-
couver, Quebec, Halifax, St. John, and a
dozen other cities could be moved upon in
succession, laid waste and remade to suit
these new proprietors of the earth and its
fulness.

In the light of what we have already seen in
Toronto, is there anything impossible in this
unpleasant picture?

It is the privilege of sensible men to reflect
upon the conditions that threaten us. If you
are not conscious that this rapidly growing
monopoly in the mercantile trade has so far
injured you, it would be wise to enquire if
your turn may not come next. Are you not
blaming on "the hard times" some of the
things directly caused by the fact that the
trade that was once diffused over the whole
city is now concentrated on a few acres in its
center, and that the profits that were once

divided among a hundred houses now enrich only two or three?

Where are the carpenters who a few years ago were almost constantly employed in building stores in all corners of the city? Some of them are idle; some have left the city; some have entered other lines of employment, causing labor to become a drug on the market and wages to fall.

Where are those who once occupied the now vacant little stores? They, too, have joined the crowded ranks of the work-seekers.

What does it profit a man that his wife can get bargains if he can no longer get work?

The price of labor and the price of all things produced by labor, watch each other with eyes that never wink, and they rise and fall together, like the face of a man and its reflection in a mirror.

There may be one bargain day in the week for the wife of the workingman, but every day in the year is bargain day for the owner of a departmental store when he buys products of labor to sell over his counters.

I am told that when a great company was organized in San Francisco to run a monster departmental store, all the manufacturing houses, real estate, loan, insurance and other companies, and private employers who expected to be injured, simultaneously discharged all their employees, and re-engaged them on an agreement to pay each one so much wages on condition that the employee should not spend or allow any part of his wages to be spent in a departmental store. This sounds like a boycott, and it would hardly be legal under our law, but I mention it because the plan was successful and the great store "played to an empty house." It shows that one city at least realized in time the danger that threatened it.

NO. IV.—THE QUESTION OF BARGAINS AND THE POSSIBILITY OF "DOING ANYTHING."

WHILE the idea prevails that the departmental stores sell goods cheaper than other stores, and that the specialists or regular dealers formerly got excessive profits from the people, it is comparatively useless to ask them to regard such stores as enemies alike to those who are in the mercantile line, engaged in professional work, owners of property, or occupied in making a livelihood in any manner whatever, by work of the brain or hand. To convince people that such stores are all-round destroyers, it becomes necessary to dispel the belief that they confer benefits upon the buying public.

This is not hard to do. Those who are in the trick know how great is the imposture practiced upon the public in regard to "bargains," and if those who read this will experiment for themselves and think seriously, they will at once discover that departmental stores have humbugged the public in brazen fashion.

You often hear people say: "If I can buy an article for 60 cents in one place why should I pay a dollar for it somewhere else?"

To this it may be answered that it is possible for circumstances to warrant one in paying the extra forty per cent. A perfectly honest man will not feel free to buy a dollar article for 60 cents if its cheapness is due to the fact that it has been stolen or smuggled. A perfectly sensible man will see no advantage in buying a dollar article for 60 cents if its cheapness is due to the fact that it is not the dollar article at all, but an adulterated substitute. The same perfectly sensible man will not regard it as a bargain if he gets a genuine dollar article for sixty cents, if the forty per cent. gained on that purchase is tacked on to another purchase made at the same time and place.

Years ago the country used to be over-run

with shoddy peddlers. One of these peddlers
would drive up to the farmhouse with a wagon
loaded with goods. He would carry into the
house two or three bales of cotton, of linen,
and half a dozen of shoddy tweeds. He would
say that a big wholesale house had failed and
that the goods had to be sold by the first of the
next month, and so they were selling at less
than half price. He would show the farmer's
wife some linen which she would recognize at
once as the very best grade, and he would
name a price only about one-third of its real
value. He would appear more anxious to sell
the linen than the tweeds, but almost reluct-
antly would show the tweeds also. The woman,
knowing the linen to be a bargain, would believe that the shoddy cloth was also really
worth three times the price asked, and so in
the end the clever swindler would sell her as
much shoddy as possible and as little linen as
possible. He would lose three or four dollars
on the linen in order to make thirty or forty on
the shoddy.

This humble itinerant, in his poor, weak way,
worked the scheme which is now elaborated by
millionaires and operated successfully in all the
great cities of the continent.

It is not necessary, nor would it be truthful,
to say that departmental stores (like the peddler) are almost altogether interested in selling
shoddy and counterfeit goods, but it is necessary and truthful to say that the departmental
stores imitate the peddler's general scheme in
that they lose money on a few trifles every day
in order to delude people into believing that
everything is sold at the same low price.

Even if they do not charge an excessive price
on any article, yet in gaining a monopoly of
trade at the cost of a few bargains they are
able every night in the year to shovel enormous profits into their vaults and exclaim:
"This has indeed been a bargain day—for us."

But there is more of the old peddler in the scheme than the mere trick of baiting a hook. We are rushing with the speed of the wind towards a period of universal shoddy. The departmental stores are not alone in dealing in inferior goods, but they are the depressing influence. If they palm off inferior goods at cheaper prices than others can sell good merchandise, the others must degrade the quality of their wares in order to sell at ruling prices.

The homes of this country are being filled with furniture that is thrown together without skill, made of inferior and uncured timber—such furniture as would have been despised fifteen years ago. It is worth no more than it costs.

Spools are sold at bargain prices, but you may note that the hole through the center of a spool grows ever bigger and the core of the spool ever fatter. A purchaser gets a bargain in spools, but does he get a bargain in thread? With satchelfuls of spools, bargain-hunters exclaim in admiration: "Well, I don't see how they do it!"

In the investigation now being held by the Legislature of Minnesota (Premier Hardy will please make a note of this), a dealer in wallpapers affirmed in his evidence that he had been approached by a paper-maker who offered to make "bargain rolls" for him, the same as he sold to departmental stores—that is, wallpaper with thicker wooden cores and three or four yards less wall-paper on each roll.

Toilet-paper is also rolled specially for bargain-hunters—rolled so loosely that it can be squeezed almost flat. It looks as big, but contains very much less paper. That done in pads is sometimes made containing eight hundred sheets instead of one thousand.

Vinegar has become so watery in the past two years that it is often useless. If the cases within my own knowledge may be used as a safe basis, I should think that no less than ten thousand housewives in Toronto who made pickles last autumn have since been forced to throw them away because the vinegar proved not to be vinegar at all.

There used to be twenty-five sheets in a quire of notepaper. This is an interesting reminiscence.

Men's linen collars are made specially for "bargain-hunters." No laundry in the world can get a gloss on them, for the trick of "doing them up" is known only to those who do up the public and can do up anything on earth. A five-cent collar is generally worth five cents and no more, just as a twenty-five-cent collar is worth its price.

A drug is advertised at "5c. an ounce, regular price 15c." The real fact is that the regular price of that drug in drug stores is only 10c. per ounce. The adv. seems to show a big bargain, and there may be a bargain for the one day, but the point is that the adv. informs thousands and thousands of customers that the regular price of that drug is 15c., and so if it is sold on other days at 12c. or 13c., people will still think they are getting a bargain in drugs, whereas the losses of bargain day will be recouped several times over. The man or woman who can "break even" with a departmental store after playing its own game on its own ground for a year, is mighty clever, and most people are far from clever in this new style of gambling.

* *

Out of their own mouths let us judge them.

Charles Austin Bates of New York is an advertising expert. He has just issued a book entitled Good Advertising, which is intended for those who write advertisements. He devotes a big share of its pages to an explanation of "Advertising a Department Store." He does not write in opposition to such institutions, but as the promoter, as the man who booms them. He is the man who inspires the clever American experts who write advertisements for the departmental stores of Toronto. He tells how he took charge of a departmental store's advertising business and made it boom.

On page 344 he says—(and every man and woman in this city and province should read this and grasp its meaning):

The responses in the house furnishing department brought joy to my soul. In six months the average business increased thirty or forty per cent. As the direct result of advertising a certain "sale," the department was crowded to overflowing, and in two days about $800 worth of goods was sold, out of which $90 worth was of the items advertised, and on which the actual net loss was $9. The rest was sold at regular prices at a good profit.

Shade of the departed peddler! In this case only $9 was lost on the "linen," while $710 worth of other goods was sold at "a good profit," not to an unsophisticated farmwoman, but to the crowds in a big city.

On page 352 he says in reference to the advertisements of a big New York house :

To look at the advertisements every day, it would seem that they never sell anything at regular prices, but this, of course, is only seeming.

He says this with the greatest possible admiration, leading up to it with the statement that "the method of offering bargains is one of the best trade-bringing plans that I know of." He had already shown in the extract from page 344 that it costs practically nothing.

Here is another tip from prolific page 344:

Suppose you advertise a "five-inch glass nappy." It doesn't tell a reader anything—a woman especially. She can't tell how big five inches are anyway; but just say, "large imitation cut-glass fruit saucers at thirty cents a dozen," and get your packers ready.

The women who are deluded by these people become their sport! There is no doubt about it; the whole thing is organized into an exact science, this hood-winking of the people. They study it ; they trade tricks. Here is another tip for writers of departmental store advertisements, page 345 :

Be pleasant. Throw in a little joke—a light and

piquant sentence or saying occasionally, just to liven
things up a bit.

Of course. Why not? A joke, a light and
piquant sentence costs really less than even
wooden nutmegs. Throw a whole lot of 'em in.

Speaking about shoe "sales," he exposes the
trick:

We cut the price from $1.35 to 98 cents and adver-
tised it very strongly, at the same time putting in an
item about the best-selling canvas shoe we had at
regular price—$1.50. We didn't lose any money on
the first item, and it brought in lots of people, to
whom a great number of the other styles of canvas
shoes were sold.

The people are treated like a great shoal of
fish in the water. The man on the bank puts a
worm on the hook and casts it in—the fish
naturally rush at it, and, instead of getting the
worm, are themselves gathered in, carried
away and fried at leisure.

* *
*

Many say that nothing can be done. "Real
estate values in Toronto have been depressed
to the extent of $25,000,000, and at least $10,-
000,000 of this is due to the influence of departmental stores, but—there is no remedy, nothing
can be done." So people talk.

It would be a very strange thing, indeed, if
nothing could be done. Here are some facts
that may form the basis of action. We shall
not suggest in this issue the remedies that
may be applied, but will be content to convince
the public that something can and must be
done. Let the public take hold of the matter,
spread knowledge, and the remedy will come
very soon. Here are a few points that members of the Legislature and the City Council
should carefully consider:

(1). If a man with a torch had started at the
Don bridge and burned down every third building he came to on Queen street until he reached
High Park, he would not thereby have destroyed as much property as departmental
stores have already done in this city. A neces-

sary building if burned down will be built again, but a building that is rendered unnecessary is worse than ashes.

(2). A departmental store by losing money in one line and making money in fifty other lines, can ruin all opposition in that one line. In furs, let us say, it can lose five or ten thousand dollars by selling for less than cost for a time, and thus crush all fur dealers, and then, with the monopoly of business purchased at this outlay, can raise prices and win back ten times what it lost. The scheme is to ruin all retailers in rotation and own the trade of the city and province. Should any man or set of men, however great their capital, be free to operate thus?

(3). Newspapers are carried free through the mails at the public expense, yet wherever they go they are the canvassing agents of these ruin-working institutions. Parcel-post and book-post regulations made to suit a previous condition of affairs, assist these monopolies to the damage of all the towns in Canada.

(4). Towns are now permitted to impose a license upon a transient trader who wishes to rush off a stock of goods and then flit to another town. In some places the license is almost prohibitory. In what way is the departmental store of Toronto less of an injury to a town in which it does business by mail and express, than the man who rushes in and slaughters a stock?

(5). Is the departmental store man entitled to rank as anything more than a transient trader even here in Toronto? One store when burned out some time ago claimed to have had a stock worth $500,000, yet that stock was only assessed at $60,000. Another of these stores claims to carry a stock worth $1,500,000, yet on being assessed at $400,000 it secured a private enquiry before the County Judge and had the assessment reduced to $100,000. The W. A. Murray Co., (not so far a departmental store), had its

stock insured for $373,000, which may be called
75 per cent. of its value, and so it was worth
$504,000, yet I find that it was only assessed at
$75,000. Departmental stores claim that they
have not paid for all their stock, and are only
taxable on what is paid for. Those goods are
here doing business, and why shouldn't they be
taxed? They compete with goods that are paid
for and are taxed. They are protected from
thieves by our police and from fire by our
brigade, and why should the maker in Ger-
many be allowed to sell goods through our
departmental stores on allowing them a commission without being taxed? By their own
showing departmental stores seem to be ware-
houses of foreign goods—they seem to be selling foreign goods on commission.

(6). If, however, these stores are not merely
handlers of goods owned by German and other
foreign magnates, and if the assessor once a
year can only catch $100,000 worth of assessable
goods in a stock worth a million and a half, and
if three million dollars' worth of goods is
turned over annually, does it not follow that
that store should be visited, assessed and taxed
eight or ten times a year?

(7). The statement is made (and a Legislative
Commission could discover whether this and
other statements are true) that a Toronto
departmental store has tried to induce a local
bicycle maker to produce wheels that it could
sell at $25 and make a profit. When he refused
to manufacture anything so inferior, it is said
he was asked to make wheels at $25 each and
the store would sell them at the same figure.
He still refused, and no doubt some foreign
firm is making wheels to be bargained here in
Toronto. What does this mean? Is it not
plain that public confidence in local bicycle
makers and handlers is to be overthrown, that
people are to be made to believe that bicycle
men are robbers and only departmental stores

are honest? Are the thousands of people hwo work in our bicycle factories and the thousands who have put up a share of the millions of money now interested in the local bicycle trade, to be destroyed in order to yield an advertisement to a departmental store and to keep one cheap foreign factory busy? And who says we have no defence against so vast a scheme of destruction? Yet men and women who depend on the bicycle business for their bread and butter spend their money in departmental stores. And it is the same in scores of other lines. Was there ever such a tragi-comedy?

(8). In Chicago the City Council unanimously passed a resolution calling upon the Legislature of Illinois to confer power upon the city of Chicago to exact a graduated scale of license fees from departmental stores, as follows :

DEPTS.	LICENSE.	DEPTS.	LICENSE.
1	$ 100	9	$ 25,600
2	200	10	51,200
3	400	11	102,400
4	800	12	204,800
5	1,600	13	409,600
6	3,200	14	819,200
7	6,400	15	1,638,400
8	12,800	16	3,276,800

In publishing this I do not necessarily endorse the idea just as it stands, but it shows that the evil exists elsewhere and is not regarded as beyond the reach of a drastic remedy.

(9). A despatch from Albany, N. Y., says: "Senator Guy has introduced a bill providing that no person or firm shall advertise that they have any peculiar advantage in price over a competitor, such advertising being deemed a design to deceive the public. The bill is aimed to stop bargain-day advertising."

(10). The Legislature of Minnesota is conducting an investigation which is publicly laying bare the whole iniquity of departmental stores —their depressing influence on real estate, on the wages of laboring people, on the quality of merchandise and the unfair, if not criminal,

power enjoyed of crushing to the death one
line of trade after another. A remedy will be
devised.

And now, before closing this chapter, I wish
to warn the cities of London, Hamilton, Guelph.
Brantford, Peterboro' and others, that it is
easier to keep out departmental stores than to
get them out once they are in.

To those country editors who are discussing
the war in Crete and the famine in India, I
would say that there has now begun a war
against departmental stores that is more important to them than the war in Crete, and
that if they do not carry themselves bravely in
the fight there will result a famine much more
important to them than the one in India.

*The Department Store is a scheme whereby
capital makes the greatest profit out of the
greatest number.*

THE daily newspapers of Toronto preserve vacant minds on the question of departmental stores. They witness the great tragedy and give no sign of interest. They seem to think that they are not concerned in the injury that is being wrought.

The *World* came out with a fight against the departmental stores. Many good articles were written and published. The ruin that was being done in Toronto was depicted with much truth and feeling. But the *World* dropped the fight, and instead began to publish the big advertisements of these all-gobbling monopolies.

The *News* made a fight against departmental stores and demonstrated that they were very evil things, but the *News* dropped the fight and instead began to publish the big advertisements of these all-gobbling monopolies.

The other Toronto daily papers have secured a share of the advertising funds of such stores without having to tell the truth about such places, their methods and the ruin they work.

Newspaper men have better opportunities than others to know of the damage being done to Toronto and the towns of the province by departmental stores, and I feel safe in saying that eight out of ten newspaper men in Toronto are opposed to departmental stores, knowing them to be great gambling institutions devoted to the humbugging of the masses and to the ruining of the shopkeepers of the city. They know that the departmental store is the mother of sweat-shops and of a very large progeny of evils that have recently begun to infest life in Toronto. There is probably not a newspaper in the city whose best writers would not jump at a chance to rouse the city and the province from the hypnotic sleep in which they lie while being plundered.

But newspapers are commercial enterprises. Chivalric notions may prevail in the editorial rooms, but not in the business offices.

As commercial enterprises, then, if all the loftier pretenses of journalism are to be openly abandoned, where do the newspapers stand in the matter?

Ten years ago the *News* (as I am informed on good authority) used to derive over five thousand dollars a year from the advertisements of merchants on Queen street west of Bay. To-day, practically every dollar of that has been cut off.

Ten, or even five years ago, the *World's* collector used to go west on Queen as far as Spadina, even to Bathurst; now he scarcely needs to step off Yonge street.

The *Telegram's* business shows the same change. Queen street has been made like a stream of water, down which everything has floated until it reached Yonge street, and there everything has congested and piled up mountains high.

On Saturday, March 6, 1886, eleven years ago, the *Globe* was a sixteen-page paper and contained forty-three columns of display advertisements, exclusive of patent medicine and foreign announcements. Among the leading advertisers in that issue of the *Globe* I notice:

Jaffray & Ryan.
Williamson & Co.
Edward McKeown.
T. Thompson & Son.
H. A. Neilson & Co.
Ewing & Co.
Woltz Bros. & Co.
Withrow & Hillock.
Samson, Kennedy & Co.

Where are these firms and the hundreds of others of eleven years ago that I could string out in a row if the facts were not known to everybody? Some of these firms quit business; H. A. Neilson & Co. moved to Montreal; most of them " failed."

Last Saturday's *Globe*, March 6, 1897, was a 28 page paper, and (if we leave out the bicycle

and mining advertisements, which are extra-
ordinary) we find that the *Globe* only had 53¼
columns of advertisements. This means that
although the *Globe* has nearly doubled its size, has
almost doubled its circulation, and is published
in a city that has, in those eleven years, almost
doubled its population, yet its ordinary advertising patronage has only increased from 43 to
53¼. While the city, the size of the paper and
the circulation of it, have doubled, or nearly so,
the actual number of its advertisers has de-
creased, as shown by a comparison of those two
issues, eleven years apart. In the 53¼ columns
of advertisements in last Saturday's issue, W.
A. Murray & Co. had almost 4 columns; T.
Eaton & Co. had 2 columns; F. X. Cousineau
had 1 column. These were big advertisements
by big stores. Among the other advertisements
were many suggestive of the times, and I
should begin by saying that Mr. Cousineau advertised the stock of

McMaster & Co., *liquidation.*
Then came

Block & Co., *closing out sale.*
G. & J. Brown Mfg. Co. (Ltd.), *in liquidation.*
J. Sutcliffe, *giving up business.*
Suckling & Co., *dress goods auction.*
    "   "   *stock 562 Yonge street.*
    "   "   *stock from Kingston.*
    "   "   *stock from Windsor.*
    "   "   *stock from Wingham.*

It is not nice to talk shop, but there will be
no shop to talk about after a while. Seigel,
Cooper & Co., on opening in New York, received immense favors from the daily press,
but after the great opening week, when the
newspapers called for advertising contracts,
they were told that Seigel, Cooper & Co., of
New York, had no use for newspapers. Instead of advertising they intended to sell a
great many things every day for less than cost,
and so send away an army of women daily
advertising the store by word of mouth.

When the trade of the city has once been made to flow, with the strength of Niagara, in one direction, and like the whirlpool circles around one spot at the core of the city, the newspapers will be told that they have served their turn and will be thrown aside like old shoes.

The departmental stores will then issue daily catalogues, enlivened with funny pictures, telegraph despatches, city news, short stories, continued stories. Already one departmental store in Toronto has secured advice about the publishing of a daily newspaper. If the daily press of Toronto assists three or four monopolies to crush out all opposition—and say what you will they are accomplices in the crimes of bargain days—their own turn will come, and the thousands who are now underfoot and the thousands who are being overthrown will neither be able nor willing to stand by that institution which we call the "legitimate" press.

Seigel, Cooper & Co., on their opening day in New York, sold bicycles at $20 each for which they had paid $90 cash. They sold thousands of wheels, on each one of which they lost $60. Their opening sale cost them perhaps two hundred thousand dollars—that is in lieu of newspaper advertising.

I am convinced that several influential newspaper men in Toronto are "almost persuaded" by their own knowledge of the facts to throw down the gauntlet to departmental stores. The Toronto Board of Trade could cause them to act now if the Board would take up the question.

Some dealers have associated in a demand that makers of certain articles shall refuse to sell to departmental stores on pain of being boycotted by all regular dealers.

Don't try to dig a well with a teaspoon. Don't be content to make war in so small a way. Train all your guns. Call out the reserves.

Let the local bicycle makers and the local agents of legitimate wheels whose businesses are to be damaged by the importation and sale at cost of wheels manufactured and glued together in prisons or in guy shops in the United States—let these legitimate local business men call upon each newspaper to choose which it will serve, the cause of honest business and honest wheels, or the cause of fake business and fake wheels. Let the wheelmen speak together and say : "It is preposterous that you newspaper men should expect to derive income from us and also from firms that bring in tin wheels which they sell at as good a profit as we get on ours, and advertise as being as good as ours. It is preposterous, we say again, and we are wise at last. Each newspaper may decide which it will do—our business or fake business."

If, then, such wheels are not advertised in the newspapers but are sold in the stores to people who are lured thither by other bait, let each manager of a bicycle factory call his employees together and say : "Such and such a firm has imported so many thousand cheap wheels (state whether they are prison-made or moulded instead of stamped, or built of culled parts, as the case may be, being careful to speak the exact truth, for the truth is quite strong enough) which are to be sold in this town. The purpose is to create the impression that these wheels are as good as those made by us, and that everything is sold for half what is paid elsewhere. Our business is to be destroyed in order to draw crowds to buy other goods. In view of this fact it is preposterous that any part of the thousands of dollars paid by us to our employees should be spent in buying dry goods, groceries or anything else in such a store. Every man of you must bear in mind that every dollar you or your wife spends in such a store strengthens it in its war upon us, and hastens the day when this factory shall shut down. We are not making wheels for fun. We are making them for sale. If we are attacked we must defend ourselves. We are sure that the men of this factory will see that their own interests are threatened as much as are the interests of the firm, and so we desire all employees to unite with us in signing an agreement not to spend one cent, nor allow anyone to spend one cent of our money for any purpose in any store engaged in an effort to destroy us and to impose humbug wheels upon the public."

Let everyone strengthen the hands and spur the courage of the bicycle people.

Refuse to support the newspaper that sells itself to the devil-fish. If you are forced to do business with it, do so under protest, and enter your protest every time. Gain one daily to your side; support it and withdraw your support from the others, and see what will happen.

THE manner in which business men and newspapers have taken up the fight against the new scheme whereby capital seeks to get a monopoly of all the avenues that communicate between the producer and consumer, is most encouraging. Letters are coming in from nearly every town between Montreal and Windsor, and presently an army of defence will have been organized, with local camps in every town and village that is not wholly resigned to its fate.

Right here it is not out of place to devote some space to those men who admit all the evils that are charged against departmental stores, bid us God-speed in our efforts, but say: "You can't really do anything." These people are worth reasoning with because they are honest, and I hope they will begin over again and think the matter out from the very basis of it, on into the future as far as they can see. It is important that they shall be won over, for they do the cause more harm than any other class. "You might as well try to turn the St. Lawrence from its course," they say. It seems to me that that simile might be improved.

Those of us who have gone into this crusade might better be described as trying to *keep the St. Lawrence in its channel* and to defeat those who have dammed up the stream at a given point in order to inundate all the country above that point and to make an arid waste of all the country further down stream. To keep up the simile, it might be added that some very extensive and wonderful dyking has been done in Holland. The sea rolls as it likes along the sea-bottoms, but Holland belongs to the Dutch. The Don River twisted its way into the city over a course like the writhings of a snake—its channel was almost as crooked as the ways of that trade which we assail—but we straightened that channel. If, therefore, we look to the rivers or the sea for encouragement we find it.

Suppose that a man claims that departmental stores cannot be abolished, yet even then he should join with us, for if we cannot do that, we can at least do these things:

We can make the departmental store pay a tax bearing the same just relation to the business done as the taxes formerly paid by other stores bore to the business done by them.

We can regulate the employment of children in departmental stores, as we have done with regard to factories.

We can, in the interests of the human family, make it imperative that girls and young women, if employed in such stores, shall be paid sufficient wages to buy food and clothing.

We can amend our postal laws so that the mail cars shall not be the delivery wagons, the postman shall not be the messenger boys, nor the postoffice staff the shipping-clerks of departmental stores, whilst our mail service is maintained by the Government and run at the cost of an enormous annual deficit.

We can see to it that the advertising matter of departmental stores shall pay its own way as it travels through the country, and not remain as now a charge and burden upon the state.

We can put a check upon the mendacity of those who issue advertisements calculated to injure or destroy other places of business, at least requiring that an advertisement shall be a valid basis of contract and not merely an irresponsible trick.

We can insist upon and secure a legislative nvestigation into the entire methods of departmental stores, so that if evasions of existing regulations are common or if practices are in vogue that require new regulations to protect the purchasing public, remedies may be applied. This investigation could disclose what effect, if any, the new craze for "cheapness" has had upon the number of inches in a foot, the number of feet in a yard, the number of ounces in a pound. If there is any difference of opinion as to whether bargains should be sold by avoirdupois or apothecary weight, the Commission could definitely settle that point.

If that Commission discovers that departmental stores make a dead-set against special dealers in some line of trade, making misstatements of values and combining all interests in one endeavor to crush out those particular dealers so that they may occupy an undivided field, this must rank as a conspiracy and a misdemeanor.

There are many things to be done, and even those who say that departmental stores have come to stay and that it is impossible to pull them up by the roots, must admit the immediate need of some action to protect the people from the consequences of their unthinking covetousness.

I am told that many who used to avail themselves of market excursion rates to Toronto are quite indignant because that privilege is now denied them. Take the town of Whitby and the country surrounding it, and study out the whole case—any other town will answer as well, Brampton, or Georgetown, or Oakville, or even those towns lying one hundred miles farther away, from which people order goods by mail instead of dealing at home. But let us consider Whitby and its environments in order to get a concrete case.

The residents of that town and the farmers around about it should pause to consider what they are doing. Fifteen years ago a farm lying one mile from Whitby was worth $100 an acre or more. To-day the same farm could not be sold for more than $60 or $65 an acre. It is the fashion to ascribe this to all sorts of fancy causes—generally some political error is charged with having depressed the value of farm lands, but have we not got a much nearer and more natural explanation? When buying a farm a man likes to get one fronting on a main road and as near a good market as possible. That farm one mile from Whitby was one mile from a good market fifteen years ago; to-day it is twenty-eight miles from a good market. For fifteen years the owner of that farm and the owners of adjoining ones have been building up a town twenty-eight miles distant and tearing down the town whose juxtaposition and conveniences once made those farm lands worth $30 or $40 an acre more than lands situated a few miles further back in the country. Not only this, but people resident in the town of Whitby and owning property there or earning a livelihood there, have aided in pulling down the town and reducing it to the status of a mere emergency market. The local merchants have been used when goods were wanted on credit; the cash has been carried away or sent away. Let me say again, I only use Whitby as an illustration, and not because it has suffered more than other places.

In a certain town that I could name a merchant tailor one day entered a book store and priced a certain book. "Two-fifty!" he exclaimed. "You just wait until I show you something." He crossed to his shop and came back with the same book, which he had secured on bargain day at a Toronto departmental store for $2. Two weeks later the stationer entered the tailor shop to get a suit of clothes. He asked the price and secured a sample of cloth. A week later he entered the tailor shop in a new suit which he had secured in a Toronto departmental store, and invited the tailor to become enthusiastic over the "bargain" he had secured. It requires only a very little reasoning power to argue out the results of such methods upon any town in Ontario. But there are many who want to buy away from home and expect to retain the custom of their neighbors. They should be pulled up with a sharp jerk.

To the man who works for a wage:

YOU have probably reasoned it out thus: "If I get so much per week, and if departmental stores enable me to buy more goods in a week or in a year than I could formerly buy with the same amount of money, then it stands to reason that departmental stores are a benefit to *me*, however injurious they may be to others."

This appears to be sound. There is nothing to be gained by shirking any point of this question, and I do not think that it is necessary to shirk anything or to hurry past any point that can possibly be raised.

If you are a carpenter, or a bricklayer, or a stonecutter, you know that building operations have practically ceased in Toronto. If you are a plasterer, a gas-fitter, a paper-hanger, you know that the town is dead in your line of work. Why? Because you and your wife, your neighbors and their wives, have begun dealing in one store, instead of scattering trade over a hundred or a thousand stores. So far as your trade is concerned there is only need for one store, and it is already built. Those who work at any branch of the building trade are, then, entitled to buy goods cheaper than they used to, for they have sold out their means of gaining a livelihood in order to centralize trade and cheapen the cost of housing goods. But what will you do now that your occupation is gone? There is no bargain day on which you can get everything you want for nothing at all.

It may be argued that if the business of a hundred stores is done under one roof, the saving in rent and taxes will enable the proprietors to make as large a profit as others while selling at lower prices, yet you, who make your living in the building trade and are now cast aside as useless, can scarcely consider that you have gained anything. You have something to sell.

and there are things you want to buy. That
which you have to sell is your labor—you cannot sell it at the old price ; you can scarcely sell
it at any price. Instead of a skilled mechanic,
you are, or soon will be, a laborer ready to take
a day's work at any odd job.

But suppose that you are not interested in
the building trade. Most people admit that the
new order of things has destroyed the prospects
of three classes : the shopkeeper, the owner of
small store-properties, and those who lived by
building houses and stores to do the trade of
the town before departmental stores came here.
Some say that what these classes lose the general public gain.

I would point out that there is no law stipu-
lating that this "gain" shall go to the public.
It is not at all absurd to imagine that
this gain goes where a great many
profits have gone in similar cases : into
the vaults of monopolists. Let us trace it
out. Who gets the gain from the concentra-
tion of trade in the hands of a few men ? Not
the bricklayers, stonecutters, carpenters,
plasterers, and others who work in the building
trade, for though their wives may have got a
few things called bargains, the husbands have
lost their employment. The man who works,
exchanges his labor for the things that he
needs ; and if his labor is made valueless, he
can get nothing that he needs.

Who, then, gains ? The general public ; the
very general public ! In Canada every man is
interested in some profession or trade—either
because he devotes his energies to a particular
profession or line of trade, or because he has
money invested in one thing or another. "The
general public" is a term that means workingmen, tradesmen, and professional men and
their families. That tradesmen are injured
because the retail trade of the city is, by a
clever game of hocus-pocus, being centralized

in a few stores, no one will dispute. I showed
last week that $3,701,000 had in the past few
years been withdrawn from use in Toronto
by firms that either failed or retired from
business. It has also been shown that real
estate values, at the lowest estimate, have been
reduced in Toronto to the extent of $10,000,000
by the centralization of trade ; so that the pro-
perty-owning part of the "general public" have
not "gained" by the new order of things. The
class of people called "clerks" have not benefit-
ed, for clerks who formerly received $12 and $15
per week are only paid from $4 to $7 in the
departmental stores. An experienced salesman cannot even get a situation at $7 per
week, because his neighbor's daughter gets the
position at $3 per week.

The "general public" begins to dwindle
away. Professional people and working people
who are not interested in the building trade,
are about the only ones left. The loan companies and the banks, with all their employees,
are not "gaining," because their customers are
going under ; houses and lands are falling back
on the hands of loan companies that don't want
such houses and lands. If a good year's business is not done, the salary list is pared down.
There is one man in Toronto who now owns
one hundred and seventy-five stores and
houses, although he didn't build or buy one of
them (only the one he lives in). On the others
he loaned money at fifty per cent. of their
value. The salesman who is offered only $5 a
week will decline it if he can get into an insurance office, or a loan company or a law office,
even at less pay to start with, for he will expect
a better future. Therefore, bookkeepers and
office hands, in any line of business whatever,
are finding that expert penmen and arithme-
ticians are looking for positions and are ready
to accept very humble salaries. Only those
office men whose services are peculiarly deli-

cate and valuable can withstand the general
downward tendency caused by the fact that
girls and boys are now doing men's work in
handling the retail merchandise of Toronto.

Clerks, then, in all kinds of offices, as well as
in stores, are feeling, or soon will feel, the evil
of which property-owners and shop-keepers
complain, and so are not "gainers." Who are
the gainers? Where are we to look for the
"general public" which benefits by centralization of trade?

Not the lawyers, for any lawyer who cares to
let the cat out of the bag will tell you that
things are in a bad way with many in the profession. I have been told of one case where a
very well known lawyer admitted that while
his income usually ran up to about $5,000 a
year, it fell away in the year 1896 to about $700.
And if three or four firms grow so powerful
that no man dare quarrel with one of them,
however injured in a business transaction, for
fear that all the powerful departmentals will
unite to crush out the man and his factory or
foundry or mill, there will be less and less for
lawyers, and much less for the laboring men
who toil under taskmasters who are themselves beneath the lash of a monopoly.

The clergy of the city are not "gainers,"
because the finances of the churches of the
city are in most cases deplorable. You cannot
impoverish the people without injuring anything supported by the voluntary contributions
of the people.

Are the working people, then, "gainers?"
It must be admitted that those engaged in any
and every branch of the building trade are
seriously injured. Consider other lines. In a
previous article it was shown that all those
engaged in the making or putting together
of bicycles are to be injured by the departmental stores selling cheap foreign-made wheels
at the cheapest possible price, in order to delude

the people into the belief that the departmental
stores undersell everybody in everything. There
are only so many wheels wanted in Canada in
this year of 1897. The success of any local
firm's business this year will regulate its out-
put for 1898. Well, then, cheap foreign wheels
sold here at the cheapest possible price to boom
any firm's business in dry-goods and groceries,
work three injuries : (1) Each wheel goes to a
man who thinks he gets a bargain, but only
gets as much value as he pays for ; (2) Each
wheel sold spoils the sale of a wheel by a legitimate maker or dealer ; and (3) Each wheel
sold tends to limit the out-put of Canadian-
made wheels next year, so that the factories
will run short-handed at the end of this season
and manufacture fewer wheels for next season.
Men who earn a living in bicycle shops are to
be injured in a way that no reduction in the
price of cayenne pepper or glass nappies can
make good to him.

There is no mechanic who is not under the
same menace.

The agent of a departmental store will go to
a furniture factory in Toronto or in one of the
towns of the province, and offer a certain price
for so many tables of a certain kind. " Make
us two hundred of those tables at sixty cents
apiece. I'll pay you $20 now and the remaining
$100 will be paid you the moment the tables
are ready for delivery." " Why, sixty cents
will hardly pay for the lumber ; we can't make
'em for sixty cents." " You can't ? Well, you
don't have to. Somebody else will—good-day."
" Hold on," says the furniture man. He gets a
pencil and paper, figures on lumber culls, only
one coat of the cheapest varnish, and any possible reduction in the wages of workmen—in
order to see if he can rattle up a table for sixty
cents. " Can't you pay sixty-five cents apiece
for 'em ?" " No. Blank & Blank are making
us two hundred at sixty cents apiece, and we'll

give 'em this order if you don't want it. Why,
man, we're going to pay you sixty cents for that
table—we're going to handle it, advertise it
extensively and sell it for 52 cents, eight cents
less than we pay you." "I'll do it." Then he
gets to work—he becomes an artificer in rub-
bish; cuts wages down, grinds, twists, turns,
writhes, in an endeavor to make those tables
for the money.

The women who buy them take them home
for the parlor, but find them not good enough;
put them in the kitchen, where they prove to be
not strong enough, and so they soon land in the
attic. But they have served their purpose;
they have caused a host of people to rush
to the departmental store, where, after seeing
the "cheap" tables, not one in twenty will buy
the "bargain," but buy other things sold at
prices which enable the firm to win back
twenty times as much as it loses on the tables.

But where do the workmen come in? Those
who made the tables very likely had their
wages cut down on the job. Other furniture
makers and dealers have been injured. Trade
has been drawn into a store where the union
scale of wages in furniture-making and everything else is cut away and utterly denied.
Hundreds of thousands of people have been
told in print that a first-class and charming
parlor table can be had for 52 cents. The whole
furniture business is demoralized. To get even
with some rival, each furniture maker, when
approached with a request to produce some
flimsy imitation furniture at a starvation
figure, accepts the offer, and so the departmental store agent, operating over the whole
field of industry, sets maker against maker
and depresses the whole field and crushes
workingmen beneath a constantly increasing
demand to manufacture goods at less cost.
Every workingman knows that when a con-
tractor finds he is going to lose, the very first

thing he does, in attempting to save himself, *is to cut wages down a little finer than they were.*

I don't care what a man's occupation may be, if he earns his living by the work of his hands or the activity of his mind, he either has already felt, or will very soon find, that his own trade or profession "is on the list." The department- mental store carves a little off every man's stature. Like the customs duties it makes its levies indirectly, and many are not conscious of the tax and do not know just why they are worse off than they used to be.

* * *

In Chicago the Knights of Labor sent a dele- gate to the meeting against departmental stores, with instructions to say that the organized labor of Chicago was heart and soul with any movement to repress the operations of departmental store monopolies. They realize there that wage-earners are now, and will be, the greatest sufferers from the system. Let the working people of Toronto figure the thing out—each man figuring out the effect on his own trade, and that of his next-door neighbor.

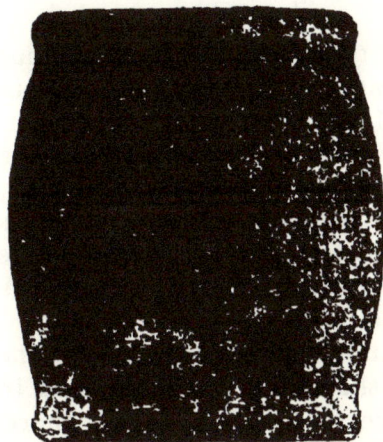

HERE we have a little thing that serves as an object lesson. It looks like a miniature hogshead, or a nail-keg. But it is not. Perhaps you would never guess what it is, this thing with the bulging sides. Well, it is an empty spool—a departmental store spool from which the thin layer of crochet silk has been removed. The great big fat piece of wood, of which this is an exact photograph, was purchased in one of the departmental stores in Toronto about two weeks ago. Imagine that corpulent piece of wood with a little string of crochet silk carefully wound around it—how big, how imposing a " spool of silk " it would seem! It wouldn't take much silk thread to bulge on that spool, for the obliging wood does all the bulging that is needed. One thin layer of thread over that wood is all that is needed to please the eye. Gazing upon its fat dimensions, noting the " bargain " price — how the bargain-hunters must have struggled to get the coveted bargain!

This fat bit of wood, upon which crochet silk was wound, illustrates the whole trick of running departmental stores. The people are jollied, cajoled, and treated to all kinds of optical illusions. Everything that possesses a wooden core gets more wooden core than it knows what to do with. Everything that is hollow has wind pumped into it to make it puff out and look big. Things are not, according to the old idea, put in shelves and

drawers to keep them clean and fresh, but
everything is spread out to its fullest to create
the impression of a big stock. The departmental store works the trick played by the
traders who spread out glaring red shawls,
ribbons, beads and cewgaws before the Indians
in the early days, telling the chiefs things
they didn't need and getting from them the
lands that they did need.

The departmental store proceeds on the
assumption that the public wants nothing in
particular and everything in general; therefore they show everything, in gorgeous and
abundant disorder, one thing priced away up
and the next thing priced away down, and, in
the din of steam-organs, squeezing, crushing,
clutching at the things that others are clutching at, the half-mad multitude tries to appear
sane and to buy shrewdly. Once home again,
each purchaser pretends to be satisfied. It
wouldn't do for a woman to admit that she lost
her head and misspent her money. And yet
women wonder that some men gamble with
cards and at horse races. The departmental
store has introduced the spirit of gambling into
the trade of store-keeping, and it looks as
though women are willing enough to gamble so
long as the sport bears the hitherto respectable
name of "shopping."

* * *

Rev. A. H. Baldwin, last Sunday night, in
the Church of the Redeemer, spoke of departmental stores and bargain-hunters. He pointed
out with telling force a fact not yet referred to
in this series of articles, viz., that women
in their greed for bargains are driving
their own sex, and ultimately themselves and
their daughters, out into the world to earn their
own living. And it may be further said they are
making the world a harder place than it ever
was for a woman to venture into as a bread-
winner. He is reported as follows:

" Why, not long ago I saw women crushing and climbing over one another in their efforts to reach the bargains, and I heard one say to another: ' Do you want that?' ' Oh, no! but it might come in useful some day.' And so the women get their bargains, while at home, perhaps, the husband cannot pay his bills.

"*I tell you that many of you are ruining your husbands. They dare not say so at home or begin to curtail.*"

* * *

One store in this town has been selling ladders for twenty-five cents each. A correspondent tells me that that store bought two hundred and eighty of those ladders last week at 35c. each, cash down, and sold them at 25c. each, losing ten cents on each ladder, and $28 on that one item. Now, will any man or woman, outside of the Provincial Asylum for Idiots near Orillia, pretend to argue that that departmental store sold those ladders at that loss because it loved the people and liked every home to have its own ladder? Why did it touch ladders at all? These ladders had not been in the way, nor were they sold at a loss to make room. Without doubt they were ordered for the purpose. They were like the earthworms which a man goes out and digs when he goes fishing. They were bait. Does anyone suppose that when bargain day was over the store was $28 short? Not a cent short, but hundreds of dollars ahead of the game. They caught shoals of fish. They got people up those ladders and made them pay to get down.

But to view it in another light: What kind of a hardwood ladder can a man make for 35c. even if he gets an order for 280 of them? How far would you take such a ladder into your confidence? Would you use it yourself or would you make the hired man use it? This is an impersonal enquiry directed not against departmental stores but against cheap ladders.

I have known a great deal to depend upon a ladder.

A correspondent informs me that a postal clerk in a town in Ontario, not many miles from Stratford, was overheard making the statement that on that particular day he had handled seventy-five registered letters leaving the town, of which fifty-two were addressed to one department-mental store in Toronto. Plows will run where that town stands if sense does not come soon to its people.

THOSE who have gone nto the fight against the humbugging of the people carried on by departmental stores have great cause for rejoicing. The fight has only lasted about six weeks, and already between seventy and eighty newspapers in Ontario—not to mention many in all the other Provinces of the Dominion—have taken up the question and intend to keep at it until success crowns the agitation.

Mr. J. T. Middleton, M.P.P., of Hamilton, introduced his Bill in the Legislature on Monday. He proposes to permit cities containing a population of 30,000 or more to pass, on a two-thirds vote of its aldermen, a by-law imposing a special tax on stores handling more than three lines of goods.

Mr. Haycock, leader of the Patrons, said he was not prepared to declare against the principle of the bill, but he asked that it be held over until the next session, as the present one was nearly over, and the question was important.

Hon. A. S. Hardy, Premier and leader of the Liberals, said he would not say that he was opposed to the principle of the bill, but he also wished it held over until the next session. He thought the departmental store destroyed individuality as well as property. To quote *The Mail and Empire* as to Mr. Hardy's position :

He hinted that a parliamentary committee to take evidence on both sides of the question and to enquire into the wages of employees, etc., would be appointed before the next session.

The *Globe* reports Mr. Hardy as saying, among other things :

Something might possibly be done to modify the immense advantages which these stores now enjoy over the ordinary business man.

Mr. Whitney, leader of the Conservative Opposition, is thus reported in the *Mail and Empire* :

Mr. Whitney said the gravity and importance of
the subject was such that it would not be possible
to deal with it in an intelligent way with the time or
double the time at their disposal. He had strong
sympathy with the objects of the bill. Coming from
a rural constituency, he knew, perhaps, better than
members from cities, that the retail merchants
throughout the country were suffering terribly from
the system of departmental stores. The Government
would have to grapple with the question sooner or
later, and adopt some means of solving it. If the bill
had been introduced earlier in the session something
might have been done.

What does this mean? It means that on the
very first mention of the question in the Legislature the leaders of the three parties spoke in
a manner satisfactory to those who have come
forward to resist the business immoralities introduced by departmental stores. The leader
of the Patrons was not prepared to declare
against the principle of the Bill; the leader of
the Liberals was not prepared to declare against
the principle of the Bill; the leader of the Con-
servatives endorsed the principle of the Bill.

What does the postponement of the question
mean? It means that there really is not time to
take it up this session, but it further and more
particularly means that all the political leaders
will wait to see what strength is developed by
the present movement, and the Legislature
will next session be governed by the facts that
are brought out and by the strength of the
demands made for reforms.

It therefore devolves upon the newspapers,
business men, boards of trade, and town
councils, to see that every day between the
close of the present and the opening of the
next session is made use of in forwarding the interests of the cause.

* *

The *World* reported Mr. O. A. Howland,
M.P.P., as opposed to Mr. Middleton's bill, but
I find by the *Globe* and the *Mail and Empire*
that Mr. Howland favored action by the Legislature, although he desired the question to be
held over until the next session, when it could

receive proper consideration. He pointed out
that in Austria legislation had been passed.
The *Globe* quotes him as having made this
good point:

There is a question whether the economy of these
stores as compared with ordinary stores was not due
to the starving of their labor, the substitution of
female for male labor, and to a large extent to the
taking of inferior labor.

The closing word of that extract might well
have been "goods," and I would not be sur-
prised to hear that Mr. Howland had used the
word "goods."

Mr. Willoughby said that no measure of
greater importance had been raised during the
session. Dr. Mathieson said it was the old
"Song of the Shirt." Labor was ground down
so that people could buy cheaply.

Mr. Middleton of Hamilton, who introduced
the Bill, was probably the best posted man in
the Legislature on the subject. He has
spent his life in retail and wholesale trade
and is fully posted on all the humbugs played
upon the people. He knows how "bargains"
are given—knows that goods are often as cheap
in merit as in price, and that the refuse of
factories is bought up and sold at profits as
large as others get for good goods. Mr. Middleton deserves credit for introducing and guiding
the Bill. He has won a partial endorsation of
the principle of the Bill, and although it may
never pass in its present form, action is sure
at next session if the campaign is pressed
forward.

* * *

Let newspaper men everywhere, the aldermen of Toronto and the members of the
Ontario Legislature consider the case which I
am about to state and decide whether, in the
face of it, the present situation can be allowed
to continue.

A professional gentleman of my acquaintance
has a cottage in the country where he resides

in the summer   He is a great lover of flowers
and every year tries to get a finer garden than
the year before.   A few weeks ago he went as
usual to the Steel. Briggs Seed Company and
bought a great variety of seeds   About ten
days ago he read a departmental store adver
tisement announcing great "bargains in gar
den seeds." and as he read the prices he was
amazed.

"If they can sell seeds at that price and
Briggs charges what he charged me," he said.
"then SATURDAY NIGHT might as well give up
the fight"

Next day, being down town, he went into the
departmental store and bought a lot of seed
packages of different varieties and took them
home.   That evening he placed the departmental
store seed packages on one end of his writing
table. and picked out corresponding packages
(the same species) from Briggs seeds and put
them at the other end of the table.   The
number of packages was the same. yet he
found that

Steele Briggs packages had cost......... $2 10
Departmental store packages had cost..   25

This showed a tremendous difference, but he
is a thorough going man. and so he decided to
examine the seeds.   He found Briggs' much
plumper and then he counted the seeds. and
after counting several packages he found that
they contained the following average number
of seeds per package :

Steele-Briggs packages. average......... 3,000
Departmental store packages. average.. 152

In other words, one package of Briggs seeds
if opened and made into departmental store
packages would make about 19½ of such
packages.

In still other words, to get the same *quantity*
of seed that had been sold by Briggs for $2.10
would cost at the departmental store about $5.

Yet seeds were supposed to be a phenomenal bargain at the departmental store.

They were loudly advertised and people clutched at them, thinking they were getting $2.10 worth for 25 cents.

People said: "It's wonderful how they do it!" This is how they did it, and is there anything wonderful about it? The department store got double the regular price of seeds, yet they got credit for giving a big bargain. The same sort of trick is worked in many ways. Be on your guard—test the thing for yourself, if you are still one of the thoughtless multitude who are pulling the city down to enrich the Barnums of Business.

Another great point in this seed episode is that the Steele, Briggs Seed Company has its whole fortune in the business of growing and selling seeds. Its reputation depends upon the merits of its seeds and bulbs. The utmost care of skilled gardeners and floriculturists is employed, and laboriously, year after year, a reputation has been built up. Poor seeds are not sold, but are destroyed. Departmental stores don't care a rap about the seed business. If garden seeds don't prove good bait, after having been used and abused a couple of seasons, other bait will be found.

I don't think people like to be humbugged any more than fish like to be caught, but many people are as foolish as fish in the way they bite at hooks that are almost bare and easily seen if they would not jump so greedily.

* *

Just to show how wily the departmental stores are: I am told that during the "millinery openings" at the wholesale houses one departmental store reduced the prices on its millinery goods from 25 to 50 per cent., and chucked prices up again the moment the milliners had left town. Why was this done? To create the impression in the minds of out-of-town milliners that that store sold as cheap or cheaper than the wholesale houses. There was no reduction announced no bargains advertised, the purpose being to suggest the idea that such prices prevailed the year around and weren't worth mentioning in an advertisement. The fact, no doubt, is that they didn't want to sell a cent's worth at the prices—they merely wanted to plant erroneous ideas in the minds of milliners who would scatter every where and talk about and act upon what they saw.

Let me repeat what has been said before: Do not misunderstand the position of SATURDAY NIGHT on this question. We are not trying to make water run up hill, nor to prevent it running down hill; but we hold that the typical departmental store cannot possibly exist in a town where two or three newspapers are devoted to the task of recording the tricks by which it attracts and transacts business. We hold that the departmental stores which make the claim of selling goods cheaper than other stores can be tackled on that, their chosen ground, and shown to be charging exorbitant prices. This may sound strange to those who have heard so much about bargains and to those who have actually secured bargains, but wise men and women will give us a chance to present our evidence on the question. We intend to show that departmental stores

Grind their employees to starvation wages in order to sell goods cheap;

Grind labor in shops, factories, cellars and garrets in order to sell goods cheap;

Depress the intrinsic value of merchandise in order to sell goods cheap;

And then, in ninety cases out of a hundred, don't sell them a cent cheaper than elsewhere, and so get four profits instead of one.

* *

Any general theory about economy of hand-

ling does not apply in the present case. for any
economy made in the cost of housing and
handling goods (with the exception of such
articles here and there throughout a store as
are necessary for bait, and these are generally
made to order to sell at the bargain price) goes
into the profits of the company and nowhere
else

The newspapers gave a monopoly to departmental stores by selling them advertising space,
in which they could daily pound the word
" bargains " into the people. The newspapers
by daily analyzing those so-called bargains. can
expose the whole game and destroy an evil, the
extent of which they did not foresee when the
circus business was first amalgamated with
storekeeping.

THOSE who think that nothing can be done in regard to departmental stores are rapidly diminishing. Thousands still frequent those stores, yet I challenge any regular departmental store shopper to deny that there is a very marked falling away in the crowds that crush and scramble in such places on those days which with brazen audacity are still called " bargain days." The attendance at these mercantile circuses is appreciably diminishing, and trade is beginning to look this way and that, and no longer blindly follows certain lines as it had begun to do. This fact is being commented upon every day, even by the women who still shop in those stores.

Determined not to lose ground, the departmental stores are spending enormous sums of money in advertising and in sending catalogues to every town and village in the country. They get voters' lists and directories, lists of the doctors, lawyers and clergymen of the province, and send out catalogues and letters (which are considered very smooth from the point of view of American advertising experts) to all those who may be thought to have no connection with the mercantile trade in the outside towns

The zeal with which catalogues are being distributed at present shows the anxiety which fills the breasts of the men who conduct these institutions They are very greatly disturbed by the wave of sentiment that is spreading over the country from one end to the other. They will be more deeply disturbed now that their business—not only that part of it which is visible here in Toronto, but their mail order trade with thoughtless people in outside towns —begins to decrease. Not only are the crowds that flock to these stores rapidly diminishing, but from all directions comes news that people who used to buy nearly everything by mail are now dealing in their own towns and intend to do so hereafter.

As I said last week, a departmental store cannot gain or retain a monopoly of the retail trade if two or more newspapers are dedicated to the duty of exposing the tricks by which it deludes and deceives the purchasing public, the tactics by which it bullies the manufacturing classes, and the malevolence with which it depresses the earning powers of laboring men. The departmental store can only succeed while the newspapers maintain a friendly silence. When newspapers refuse to any longer accept a share of the plunder the "game is up." But if the press waits too long—if it waits until the monopolies can walk alone or until they start daily papers of their own—the fate of the press may not be pleasant in the hands of a public realizing at last that it was sold out by the newspapers at "so much per line."

* *

The case mentioned last week of garden seeds purchased from the Steele, Briggs Seed Company, (Ltd.), and seeds purchased at a departmental store, showed up the whole scheme of departmental stores. Seeds were advertised as a great bargain, and seemed to be so in the eyes of careless or ignorant people, yet, in that very thing boomed as a bargain, we showed last week that the departmental store was charging more than double the regular price of such seeds as sold in any legitimate store in Toronto or throughout the province. Let anyone who bought seeds before the last issue of our paper appeared, compare their purchase with seeds bought from reliable local dealers and they will find that they paid double the regular price. And when you verify our statements in this matter remember that this exorbitant charge was made upon a thing that was loudly boomed as a bargain. There are

many tricks beside this seed trick, nor was the
seed trick confined to one of the departmental
stores. Here is a letter received by us before
our last week's paper was printed, but too late
to appear in that issue. This refers to a different store from the one referred to last week :

A lady of my acquaintance was down town
shopping, and seeing six packages of seeds
marked up for 10c. in one of the large departmental stores, thought she was getting a great
bargain, and bought six packages and brought
them home. In the evening a gentleman
called in and, seeing the seeds which the lady
showed him as such a great bargain, suggested
that she should send across the road to the
grocery store opposite and buy a 5c. package,
which she did, and on opening the contents of
the package from the grocer's it was found that
there were more seeds than in all of the six
packages purchased from the departmental
store put together. In other words, the lady
paid 10c. for seeds in a departmental store that
she could have purchased across the road at
her grocer's for 5c., not counting car fare.

The *Evening Star* on Saturday exposed another case. A customer went to a departmental
store to get a "bargain in wool." There had
been advertised "4 oz. Berlin wool for 10c."
He took the purchase away and had it sub-
jected to official analysis. Each skein of Berlin
wool is supposed to weigh an ounce. Sixteen
of them make a pound. The purchaser got 4
skeins, but they weighed scarcely 3 oz. instead
of 4 oz. That is, sixteen of them would only
weigh 12 oz. instead of 16 oz. Here is another
bargain exposed. It is just like the seeds.
The bargain is explained by the shortness of
the weight.

The *Star* also mentions another bargain at
the same store—3 spools of sewing silk, size E,
for 5c. This is a cheap grade of sewing silk
and usually sells 3 spools for 9c. The customer
bought three and had them measured, and
instead of containing fifty yards of silk they
contained only thirty. They were twenty yards

short. The three spools instead of containing one hundred and fifty yards contained only ninety yards. That is, leaving out the wool and speaking of fifty yards as making one spool, they only sold 1 4-5 spools instead of three, as advertised. Nor is that all ; the sewing silk on being tested was found to be inferior. Size E sewing silk is required to stand a breaking strain of 14 pounds. This, when tested, snapped at a breaking strain of $3\frac{1}{2}$ pounds. The customer, then, got no bargain at all, but actually paid far too much for that sewing silk, according- ing to the prices in other stores where circus and lottery tricks are not employed. Remember now that this, like the seeds and the Berlin wool, is in regard to one of the very things that was boomed to draw custom. One would think that the departmental stores could afford to give the paltry bargains adver- tised by them without resorting to short measure and short weight in regard to those particular items, considering the abundant opportunities they have of getting even. It only shows the audacity with which a scheme is pursued once it has been successfully worked without being exposed.

Probably the reason why even "bargains" are made to pay two or three profits—perhaps the reason why good bait is no longer used, is partly because the public will now bite at any- thing, and partly because a great many city people, having discovered that average prices in departmental stores are as high if not higher than in other stores, began to systematically buy up the bargains without spending another cent there for fear of getting the worst of it. *This trick of gobbling up the bait without getting caught on the hook didn't suit the fisherman,* and so now even the bait is doctored. It is no longer safe to buy even those things that seem to be sold cheap to draw people to such stores. The

only thing to do is to make it a point of honor
never to enter such a store.

* *

There is a cheap broom that is offered for 10c.
by grocers in all parts of the city. Very few of
them are sold. A woman after trying one will
seldom buy another. The departmental stores
boom that broom at 5c. They lose nearly 3c. on
each one they sell, or 35c. on every dozen, but
t ıey sell very few of them. Yet they boom
them and women come to see them, but decide
that while they are marvelous bargains at the
price they are not quite good enough, and so
they buy something a little better. And this
is where the store gets in its tine work. The
broom that is sold all over the city for 25c. is
sold there for 30c., and the 15c. broom for 20c.,
so that while the departmental store offers to
lose 35c. a dozen on brooms that no one buys, it
makes 60c. a dozen more than grocery-store
prices on the brooms that are used in every house
in the city and province. This is how the game
is played.

THERE was at one time a condition of trade in which honesty was the best policy. A man, in beginning a mercantile career, said: "I shall build up a reputation for fair dealing. My goods shall be what is claimed for them. My word shall be as good as my bond. I am an expert in my line and I shall personally buy every dollar's worth that enters my store—I shall sample and test everything I purchase. Not a snide article shall enter here, and once I catch a manufacturer attempting to substitute inferior stuff I shall cease to deal with him. Mine shall be the best store in town. I shall hire expert salesmen -- men who know the values and qualities of different grades of goods. Buying keenly, taking advantage of all discounts, I can sell as cheaply as any other store, and my claim on the public will be that my word is as good as my bond and anything bought from me has a guaranteed value."

And so he would begin his career. In buying goods he watched the market with a keen eye. After buying goods he inspected them personally, and if inferior to sample threw them back upon the hands of the maker and closed his account with that man. His high principles purified trade. If he ever sold shoddy cloth he called it shoddy cloth, and did not advertise that he was selling "the high-class goods of a bankrupt merchant tailor." He played fair. He prospered, and when he died his son took up the business and ran it on the same principles as the father. It was an honorable house wherein a blind man could get as good value for a thousand dollars as could a man with ten eyes.

But now! Of what value to a house is a reputation for fair dealing built up by fifty years of resisted temptations and unblemished honesty? It is practically valueless, and why? What have we got in return for that honesty which is passing out of the mercan-

tile trade? We have something like a
Punch and Judy show behind every counter to
amuse the buying public so that they will not
notice that the nutmeg they get for half price
is made of wood, and so that they will not bite
their change to see if it is good money. In
return for that security which the purchasing
public once enjoyed, in return for that lost
honesty in trade, the public enjoys when shopping the music of steam-organs, and the pleasure
of walking under "thousand dollar arches of
flowers"—organs, and arches, and other vulgar
ostentations that cost a heap of money and
must be paid for out of the profits of "bargains."
To do this such a store opens a new trunkful of
tricks every day—and the tricks of any one day
would, if exposed, have forever disgraced the
storekeeper of fifteen years ago.

Am I wrong? Am I heated in argument and
saying extravagant things? Then pay no at-
tention to me but experiment for yourself if
you still deal with those who are ruining real
estate and reducing labor (although labor
doesn't quite know as yet what ails it) to por-
ridge and rice as food and brown duck as
clothes. Wait for a bargain day in tape
measures and a bargain day in scales.
Test your general dealer as you used to test
your grocer, your butcher and your baker.
That is but fair, and you can accuse me of no
unfairness in advising it. If you find that you
get full weight or full measure, or if on submitting other lines of goods to those competent
to judge, you find that you got full value in
quality, send me word, for, believe me, very
few are sending in such testimony. Surely
there can be no unfairness in making this
request. Let anyone, therefore, who really
buys a genuine article from one of the Barnums
of Business for a cent less than the same genuine article would cost in another store, kindly
send us particulars of the case.

Do those people who are not engaged in the mercantile line ever pause to consider the conditions under which trade is now done in Toronto? Those connected with mercantile trade pause long and seriously to consider the situation, but do outsiders never see cause for alarm in the condition of things, aside altogether from considerations as to whether the departmental stores can be legislated against and wiped out? What is the condition? Is it not practically true that the manager of a first-class down town store can never tell on Monday morning whether he is going to do ten thousand dollars' worth of business during the week or one hundred dollars' worth? The volume of trade is no longer regulated by the necessities of the people. Purchasers are not only lured to certain places which are not their "natural markets," but they hold themselves in readiness to rush out shopping any morning to buy things that seem to be offered for sale cheap. The housewife used to decide that she needed certain things and that she could afford to buy them, and then she would set out to purchase them. Now she never knows what she needs (or at least what she will buy) until she has read the bargain day advertisements. The result is that there must be tons of sham finery in the homes of this city where square meals are not absolutely sure. It is an old saw : *He who buys what he does not need, will soon need what he cannot buy.* It is as true of women as of men.

But trade is no longer regulated by the necessities of the people. People no longer shop for necessaries, but for the things that happen to be offered at apparent or pretended reductions in price. The honest storekeeper who adheres to legitimate methods is kept in hot water. The departmental stores keep pounding away on their tom-toms to attract the multitude, and the legitimate dealer knows that any day the vacant store next door may be occupied by a man who will put out a great sign, "Bankrupt Stock," and draw big crowds, although charging from 15 to 30 per cent. above regular prices for job lot stuff that no legitimate dealer would have handled at any price a few years ago.

I do not think that I am astray in saying that a stock of goods damaged by water and smoke can, in this city of Toronto to-day, be sold over the counter for fifteen per cent. higher prices than the same goods can be sold for if they are not damaged by fire and smoke. What I mean by this is, that the moment there is a fire in a store people decide that there will be bargains, and so they rush in and scramble for the privilege of paying more for damaged goods than they would have paid for the same goods before they were damaged. Women are not alone in this. Men go in and buy winter underclothes in April—cheap, coarse, and so large that a suit of it would hold two such men. The bargain is used as a mop before the next winter. I am told that "bargains in underclothes" make really good mops.

www.ingramcontent.com/pod-product-compliance
Lightning Source LLC
Chambersburg PA
CBHW021630270326
41931CB00008B/950